PORCHLIGHT

P.S. GLYCKHERR

atmosphere press

© 2025 P.S. Glyckherr

Published by Atmosphere Press

Cover design by Ronaldo Alves

No part of this book may be reproduced without permission from the author except in brief quotations and in reviews.

Atmospherepress.com

PRAISE FOR
PORCHLIGHT

"P.S. Glyckherr's Porchlight is a tender and evocative collection of poems that beautifully navigates the complexities of faith, love, loss, and personal growth. With her lyrical and meditative style, Glyckherr invites readers on a journey through both the divine and the human experience, offering solace, reflection, and spiritual nourishment along the way. At the heart of Porchlight is the theme of faith, which the poet presents not as a distant or abstract concept but as a constant, guiding presence. The image of a porchlight—steady, unwavering, and always shining—serves as a powerful metaphor for the divine light that remains even in our darkest moments."

-CHARNJIT GILL, AUTHOR OF *Pray Tell*

"In the journey between the darkness and life and the plea for strength to continue. Suffering loss unknown with the wisdom of the present to confront the sins of the past layer by layer. Thrusted upon the mercy seat of the divine to find peace in a life redefined. Courage, strength and grace; Oh how she persists! This work of redemption and light reminds us on your darkest night you are safe in the porchlight."

- ANDREW CLONINGER, AUTHOR OF *C6-C7*

In memory of my grandmother
(1903-1976)

CONTENTS

Porchlight	1
Empower Me, Lord!	2
The Orphan	3
Abandonment	4
The Child Inside Me	5
Simply Terrified	6
Rediscovery	7
"No Big Thing!"	8
Time to Create!	9
Closet Cabinets	10
Tiny Words	11
Crickets	12
Weather Girl	13
Divine and Human	14
Only Human	15
Grandmother's House	16
The "Piece" Maker	17
"Superstar" (Ode to a Carpenter)	18
Ode to Eugene	19
Relative Essentiality	20
The Squabble	21
The Friendship List	22
Violets	23
Feathers	24
What If?	25
A Warning for the Innocent	26
Perfect Scar	27
Tranquility	28
"Hurting People ... Hurt People"	29
Therapy for Arrogance	30
Sunglasses	31

First Kiss	32
My Heart Never Lies	33
Blessed by You	34
The Power of Roses	35
My Songstresses (For my Daughters)	36
Artists in Training	37
Teddy Bears	38
Thank You, Elizabeth Kubler-Ross	39
Borrowed but Cherished	40
Memory Address	41
Who We Become	42
Happy Birthday, Older Friend	43
No Limits to Love	44
What Love Is ... and Is NOT	45
"Storge" LOVE	46
Things Left Unsaid	47
One-on-One Time	48
Better	49
Perfect Plan	50
Ol' Nicodemus Here	51
Tangents	52
Aging With Grace	53
Faith Is My Choice	54
Have No Fear	55
Listen	56
Satisfaction	57
Patriot's Prayer	58
The Best of Me	59
Shekhinah	60
River	61
Home	62

Porchlight

Porchlight is on!
Darkness is gone –
like a brand-new day.
Your bright blue door shows me
a cozy space ... free from all harm –
where I want to stay a while,
smile at the warmth all around me
while sadness soars away!

Empower Me, Lord!

Empower me, Lord!
Inspire me, please ...
to be someone who practices
what I believe.
Thank you for easing my fears,
for drying my tears.
Please calm my anxieties.
Help me do those things
You've designed just for me.
Help me be there
for someone else in need.
Use me to help them believe!

The Orphan

Orphaned by my father
at the guiltless age of three,
he dumped us all –
my mother, brothers and me.
And without one word, he never returned!
My heart ached, and yes; it burned!
Growing up without a father
made it harder on my mother
who could not manage well on her own.
She became an orphan too –
another victim ... left alone.
Orphans are a different species, you see –
abandoned to grovel and beg
in the most humiliating ways.
Conveniently aborted outside the womb,
they constantly grovel and pay
for being ... unwanted.
Every lonely day and night,
an orphan's life is haunted.

Abandonment

Just one negative action
without regret
will erase those faces
we tried to embrace, and
replace them with
only a victim's burden
with no solutions in mind ...
just loss and lonely spaces
recklessly left behind.
Those feelings of abandonment –
like a needle threads the suture,
can wreck one's only future ...
both yours and mine.

The Child Inside Me

The child inside me asked,
"How much do You love me, Lord?"
"You are my Heart!" He said softly,
"I could not LOVE you more!"
The child inside me asked again,
"Lord, how long will You be mine?"
"As long as Heaven lasts," He said,
"And Heaven knows NO time!"
Sometimes children don't understand
these differences between God and man.

Simply Terrified

Have you ever been simply TERRIFIED?
Then and again, I am –
especially when I FLY, OH MY!
Uncertainty makes it so much worse.
Makes an old woman want to curse!
If God meant for me to REALLY FLY, then
surely, I'd have some WINGS!
I don't think He planned ahead
for this kind of irrational thing.
An iron bird? What in the world is that?
Lord, there must be a better way!
Do we really need a FLYING CHURCH
where TERRIFIED people pray?

Rediscovery

So ... I move across the game board
as though it's always my turn.
There are many other players,
but each one plays alone.
Some sleep while I drift effortlessly along.
And by no deliberate will of my own,
I float slowly in soapy suds of blue and white
with no bird or fish or angel in sight.
And as I rock on these wings, I eat, drink and
... THINK about a thousand other things,
for in 21 minutes, I will WIN this game!
When my feet touch solid, holy ground ...
when I hear the cheering voice of my child,
PEACE WILL AT LAST BE FOUND!
I will REDISCOVER and THANK God and man
for holding this plane inside their hands!

"No Big Thing!"

Like our hair and skin,
The butterfly's wings are soft and thin.
Like a scar on our skin,
or a split end of hair,
Their broken wings resist repair.
But unlike humans
when breaking our bones,
butterflies feel no pain that's known.
Still, they can't fly with a broken wing –
So, a scar or split ends?
"No big thing!"

Time to Create!

Have you ever CREATED anything?
A scratch-baked pie?
Penned a song to sing?
Have you bought the paint ...
sanded the fence, but then
washed away your fingerprints?
Are you afraid to share
what's under your hair?
Those antique marvels?
They are there ... somewhere!
We were created by GOD Himself
with tenacious talents all our own.
So, don't be shy!
You've got purpose inside ...
whether a freshly famed concerto or
a marshmallow, chocolate-cream pie!

Closet Cabinets

In my cabinets are a wealth of words –
old and scruffy ... and some absurd,
but more so revealing common sense, and
never offensive, but often intense.
Some words I've shared,
and some I won't.
You'll never read them
unless I know you care ...
how I've listened, learned and lost, and
more importantly, how I've loved –
but not without some cost.
I keep my pain locked up tightly –
in cabinets full of rhyme.
And each time I file a part of myself,
I laugh ... or sometimes cry.

Tiny Words

My own "tiny words" were twice published
next to Shakespeare, Shelley, Milton and Poe.
Like a young bird flying for the very first time,
I stretched new wings and learned to rhyme.
My tiny fountain fed their seas
from scars down deep inside of me.
I mixed myself into boundless scroll –
my "present day" with their "long ago."
My words pierced pages in tiny rows
along with Shakespeare, Shelley,
Milton and Poe.
Shared lively lyrics all my own –
though still ... today, I'm not well-known.

Crickets

Don't you just ...
REALLY DISLIKE
that cringing, crackling Cricket sound?
I think Crickets practice together
in a bubbled up, blistering
Cricket town!
Moment by moment –
that cringe-worthy beat!
Do they ever stop?
Don't they ever eat?
Somewhere in the marshlands,
Crickets are said to be ...
"The Sound of Hope!"
But I don't think it's found
in hauntingly horrible,
shuddering sounds!
They call and call
for their mate to appear,
but no mate comes forward
year after year after year ... after year!
... Now imagine the sound of those Cricket TEARS.

Weather Girl

Before the rain ...
I feel terrible, terrible, terrible pain
in every bone and every joint,
at every nerve and pressure point.
You could call me "your weather girl" –
but without "applicable" degree.
And though it may seem somewhat strange,
"My People" depend on me
to tell them it's going to rain!
Who knew the weather channel
could not outdo MY pain!
Perhaps it's just those Crickets again ...
driving me insane!

Divine and Human

HOW DO WE
begin to comprehend
anyone who is both
Divine and Human?
The wonder of such a concept
sits restless inside my mind –
turning ... twisting,
trying to reconcile
the relevance and unlimited
power and compassion
embodied and extended, and
that only ONE can claim.
His name is JESUS –
Both Divine and Human –
A Savior and a Friend –
Forever and ever and ever the same!
A GIFT beyond compare –
wrapped in ONE Holy name!

Only Human

What does it mean to be only Human?
I've been told that I am.
Philosophers have tried their best to explain,
but not one of them really can.
All Humans have a voice and a name,
and a soul that one day God will claim.
We think!
We perceive!
We do!
And sometimes it's true
that we don't know why ...
We EXIST at all!
But when we are DONE being Human,
The Divine is WHO we call.

Grandmother's House

Grandmother's house was full of love!
The sweet smell of flowers ... and baking,
a sewing machine winding thread.
Story books for reading ... and
little shoes in line at the end of her bed.
Sunday dinners were my favorite gifts!
Fried chicken, potatoes, and veggies galore!
A little music playing for extra flavor ...
a store of goodies in her candy drawer!
Crushed ice in our glasses with sodas of choice.
The Holy Bible on her table
still echoes her voice.
She prayed thanks to God for each one of us.
Grandmother's house was full of love!

The "Piece" Maker

She was a "Piece" Maker.
She pieced together the world
with her tiny, crippled hands.
There was nothing so broken
that couldn't be mended –
a torn piece of clothing ...
or even a heart.
She stitched her way through life,
loving us more than ever before.
Making a clear choice,
she listened closely to the voice inside her,
threw away her pride
and helped to recover each of our souls.
With loving pieces of herself,
she miraculously mended my world.

"Superstar"
(Ode to a Carpenter)

One superb, superlative "superstar" –
an innocent with the tone of an angel ...
and a voice that could bring me
to critical tears.
And even now, after all these years,
I listen to Karen's own heart breaking:
"God bless the Beasts and the Children.
For in this world, they have no voice.
They have no choice."
And once again, I wonder why
someone that flawless had to die so soon.
One outstanding original "superstar" –
an innocent with the tone of an angel ...
still brings me to critical tears.

Ode to Eugene

Sweet Harmonica ... haunting me.
Heart-breaking yearnings
from the great Eugene Record.
Enchanted, I am listening ... and needing
just one man to feel that way about me.
I would wipe away all pain – his and mine,
wrap my arms around him, and
never let him go!
So sorry I didn't know.
I yearned for you too –
whenever I felt blue
and yes, even now –
when I hear "Oh, Girl."

Relative Essentiality

What is appropriately basic
or pertinently key –
may not be the same for you
as what's required for me!
What is relatively crucial
or necessarily germane –
may be partially related,
but still not quite the same.
What is vital to both of us
might be indeed
SUPERFLUOUS ...
or even most irrelevant
and hardly worth all the FUSS.
So, comparatively speaking,
what is pertinently-key
depends on one's perception
of ESSENTIALITY!

The Squabble

I am not easily influenced.
I study both sides
to find my truth.
I listen to learn.
I laugh, then discern
the disparities between
wisdom and youth.
If you disagree
with my theories and
believe you're right
and I'm wrong,
study both sides
and you may find ...
we might have agreed all along.

The Friendship List

We become sensitive while growing old –
knowing all we've been told
must somehow be sifted through
to find the right or wrong ... for me ... for you.
We want to have faith in what we do –
to trust uniquely in who we are
and who we want to be,
and hold onto HOPEFUL days –
enjoying our right to be free!
So, when we tell our truths to treasured friends,
there should be no adversity!
If there's a LIST OF THINGS we cannot be
or words we cannot say,
or points of contention that will not bend –
that might muddy the water
or cause friendship to end,
then I wonder what we've really learned
from our "One Unconditional Friend."
We should feel free to share
every thrill and each concern
as well as confessing our sins.

Violets

Absent friend ...
spare your tears
for the Violet fields
you once shared with me.
Leave one there
by our willow tree where we walked,
and another one on that tattered bench
... where we talked.
Leave one all alone
like you once left me ...
then another lonely tear
blowing in the wind –
finally free.
Spare your last tear
as you toss thoughts of me aside
and tell all the fading Violets
why you lied.

Feathers

Feathers, fragile, yet fearless –
like wings soaring high
and gliding home again,
our friends are much like feathers –
free to fly away.
Why do some friends hover above
while ONE flies in to stay?

What If?

You know that I love you,
but what if I couldn't?
I know God loves me
though He probably shouldn't.
I do wonder IF or WHEN I can ever measure up
or become GOOD enough ...
when I can never become someone I'm not.
What you see here in front of you
is simply ME – just as I am, and
LOVING YOU with all that I've got!
So, when I wrap my arms around you,
I hope you know I mean it!
Otherwise, I wouldn't.
And what if I couldn't?

A Warning for the Innocent

She was an "Innocent" –
unaware of the fear she would face.
He was talented and clever –
and promised his embrace.
Then one day, anger was born
with a fist plunged through a "rectory" wall
directly in line with her face!
Slamming doors and objects thrown ...
a frenzy of insults plagued their home.
Terrible tantrums, growing hate,
a pillow once used to suffocate!
"You are MY wife!
This is MY home!
You will do what I say, or else!"
How was she supposed to respond?
"May I please live by myself?"
A small piece of Jewelry
in a tiny wooden tote
escaped his fuming fingers
once clenched around her throat ...
but it still can't be shared,
sold or given away!
It's an OLD and COLD reminder
of why she didn't stay.

Perfect Scar

All scars are reminders of where we've been.
"Fibrous tissue repairs injured skin."
Marks of "the how, the why and when" –
like the process that heals broken hearts,
damaged, wrecked and ripped apart.
When pain has no end, there is no art
to repair or paint over that lingering sting.
Joy becomes sorrow.
Birds fail to sing.
We cannot erase a loved one's face
or renew passion in a hollow space,
but we breathe again and begin to heal
when both love and pain are fine to feel.
A heart's memory scar runs wide and deep –
beneath the flesh and through muscle and bone.
Then above your mended, once-shattered heart
rests a perfect scar ... all your own.

Tranquility

In my stillness, I have wept.
No movement, no light, no sound.
I have walked in my own darkness –
no shadows, no path to be found.
Though without certain friends –
ALIVE to confide in,
MY LORD sits endlessly by my side –
where I welcome Him into my stillness
as my tears float away!

"Hurting People ... Hurt People"

A wise old woman once told me –
"Hurting people ... hurt people!"
And I had to stop and wonder:
Just what kind of rock
has this Guru been living under?
I thought about
all the bullies I've seen.
Had THEY been hurt by another?
Then I saw a bully change one day –
right before my eyes ...
when another bully bullied her, and
at last, she realized ... that
"Hurting people ... hurt people."
She had been one of those herself.
And from that day forward,
she turned into someone else.
Instead of being a bully,
she intentionally sought to be kind!
Her NEW soul became that friend
we search our whole lives to find.

Therapy for Arrogance

Have you EVER SEEN so many
arrogant character traits?
Always, "I'm the best!
I have no time to collaborate!"
"How dare YOU challenge ME!
Your mind is FULL of YOU!"
Do you ever stop and listen?
You truly have no clue!
You point out MY mistakes,
breeding billions of your own.
And when you put me down,
I hear RUDENESS in your tone.
So, if I attempt to humble YOU,
am I an "Arrogant" too?
Is therapy a cure for both of us?
I venture to presume ... that
sometimes WE are arrogant –
like the "Prickly Pear" in bloom!

Sunglasses

In the fall of 1978, I stood on a hillside –
the wind caressing my hair.
No plans except to admire a new breeze.
The past was far behind me,
and the future –
spinning new paths,
drew me into the SUN!
... and so, I put my
sunglasses on!

First Kiss

When I am old ...
and life's memories fade,
I will still remember
the shape of your mouth
and the first touch from your lips on mine.
No piece of art, no musician's tune,
not even a poet's rhyme
could reinvent a body inspired
and the reverence of my heart
in that twinkling moment of time.
The first kiss is truly a fever
of aching hunger and thirst –
a painful lust through a raging fire –
LOVE'S passion ALIVE in sinless desire.
And, like ash of lava frozen in frame –
when that first kiss ends,
we are NOT the same!

My Heart Never Lies

Is that a sparkle in your eyes I see
after a warm embrace?
Does my heart begin to beat
whenever you hold my face?
Is it the longing for your touch
after I let you go, or
the love I feel inside ...
wondering if you know
just how irreplaceable you are
to someone as grateful as I?
My heart's greatest treasure is YOU,
and my heart never lies!

Blessed by You

I am amazingly blessed
to have you in my life!
I have loved you in a way
that makes me pray for you.
And isn't it glorious
whenever introverts unite –
flying kites, unguarded
in a clear blue sky?
Never asking why
we were brought together –
just treasuring the time,
enjoying each other.
Like a poem in the making –
or sweet peace in my prayers,
YOU have ALWAYS been there.
And I am amazingly blessed by ...
YOU!

The Power of Roses

He promised her roses –
wistful white and sweet.
Ribboned altogether,
long-stemmed and quite unique.
She carried them proudly down the aisle
as this couple prepared to repeat
those elegant words inside their hearts
to make their bond complete.
White rose petals thrown about the church
before their wedding vows
had brought all guests to tears –
though it was clear ... all tears were allowed.
White roses woven through her hair
made every strand stand out.
Now those roses, pressed in a book ...
prove LOVE was never in doubt.

My Songstresses
(For my Daughters)

You may not have found fame, but
YOUR voices are famous to me!
You may not have found gold, but
GOD ordained you to sing!
Don't ever stop creating!
SWEET MUSIC is meant to be shared.
Blessings found in your Heavenly sounds
are worth ten thousand prayers!

Artists in Training

When souls are set on fire
with bullish brushes in their hands,
planting palettes of color,
focused fingers ... precision hands,
no single stroke is permanent!
Revolution is their friend!
God's artistic, kindred souls –
audacious ... and in command!
Artists are exceptional Miracles –
the Brightest Stars in a Perfect Sky ...
God's Gemstones in the Sand.

Teddy Bears

He sang a song about Teddy Bears –
"The Brown Song" I believe.
He practiced for perfection ...
no mischief up his sleeves.
I witnessed God's creation there
as he sang this song in tune.
His smile was never-ending –
JOYFUL the whole way through.
He filled our house with laughter
as he cackled "right out of the blue" –
a sound that reversed all sadness
from a heart so tender and true.
He sang a song about Teddy Bears –
"The Brown Song" I believe.
A voice forever treasured.
INSPIRATION was achieved!

Thank You, Elizabeth Kubler-Ross

We never met, yet Elizabeth knew
"Our Teddy Bear" drew ...
one flower bent over
next to the rest standing strong and tall.
Deep down inside he knew –
though he'd not been told
he would always be young
while we would grow fragile and old.
These flowers are drawn every day
by children all over the world.
Do they know their fate –
that their life will be brief
while the rest survive and wait?
We acknowledge these flowers
so sacredly bent
in memory and in honor of
LIVES bravely spent.

Borrowed but Cherished

Children are borrowed –
loaned to us by our Maker for only moments.
We are chosen –
to hold, nurture, and teach the things
we have been taught.
And though our every thought and action
are to keep them safe and secure,
our future on this rattled earth
is somehow most unsure.
When borrowed time ends too soon
and dreams rest in the past,
sweet memories of moments shared
will make each minute last.
It isn't the end. We will see them again!
The Bible shows us signs
of how we'll meet, and trade memories made
in our cherished, borrowed time.

Memory Address

I visited your memory address today
and placed a flower in your vase –
a yellow one like the sun ...
but of course, it wasn't REAL.
It was warm and welcoming
at the fountain, and I savored
those peaceful sounds.
I spoke to you as if you were there with me,
though I can only hope
you might hear or see.
Many memories of us, I must confess,
are re-lived in the quiet of your memory address.
Places and faces, and I can't forget ...
your contagious laughter
in our time well-spent.
Until we speak again in person, my friend,
I will visit your memory address often ...
and again I'll bring you lovely FAKE flowers –
for I remember you said not to pick the REAL ones ...
with God's "most perfect scent."

Who We Become

My heart is NOT just my own.
A piece of it has been left
with each soul I have loved.
Each meeting of hearts
deserves to be celebrated, applauded –
not only for how LOVE began,
but for all LOVE helps us become.
Just think about that.
We are never alone!

Happy Birthday, Older Friend

Listen closely now
to your friend from long ago.
I'm thinking of you today
and hope you'll forever know
that YOU are unique –
beyond compare!
Your friendship is
your gift – SO rare.
I pray now for you,
the "older one" –
much wiser and full of gray, and
I hope for your smile
meant just for me
on your incredibly special day!

No Limits to Love

I grew up wondering
if there were limits to love.
And if there were limits,
what TRAVESTY
would make love end?
Friends came along ...
and like some friends do,
they might stay for a while ...
then search for someone new.
But God showed up
with NO LIMITS TO LOVE!
No sin could I commit
to make HIM go away.
He reminds me every day ...
I AM LOVED, and
HE IS HERE TO STAY!

What Love Is ... and Is NOT

Love is NOT "an island
standing alone in the sea."
Love is an old grandmother
taking special care of me!
Love's NOT the "simple equation
of two halves making a whole."
Love is the Virgin Mary –
obedient and bold!
Love is NOT conditional –
like some stories we've been told.
Love can answer every question.
Surrender now and behold!

"Storge" LOVE

God says to cherish all souls in our lives.
Each one is a gift ...
a bond – tender, strong and true.
We are commanded to show our love –
the right and caring thing to do.
Devoid of mercy and devotion,
LOVE is "lifeless" when not in motion.
We must be thoughtful and kind
toward all God's children –
our fathers, mothers, sisters and brothers.
Yes, God commands us all
to LOVE one another!

Things Left Unsaid

Truth was a word easily dismissed –
like a list with no beginning or end.
The truth depended on a bottle of booze
and a bed he could choose
to avoid what was real.
You see ... he was sick inside.
Fretful fights between love and pride.
No doctor could provide a pill
nor anyone fill up those missing pieces,
scattered but never revealed.
Damaged and doubtful, he tossed in his sleep
... wanting so badly to believe.
He died one night in a hospital bed
with so many thoughts still left unsaid.
And when I think of him today, I grieve.

One-on-One Time

I've wanted to know you –
One-on-One,
but "things" got in the way.
Precious One-on-One time –
YOU know what I mean,
but perhaps another day.
Oh, you love music?
Wow ... I do too!
We might write a song together
when there's nothing else to do.
I'd love to know your thoughts
about the world we're living in.
But when could all that happen,
and how do we begin?
Have you ever wondered
about the structure of clouds
or God's vast universe?
Think of all you've been taught,
and we'll write it in a verse.
I want to know who you are –
about any battles you might have fought.
What knowledge that would be!
Quite an ingenious thought!

Better

To belong is to thrive –
to make ourselves whole!
To feel completely ALIVE ...
with whatever begins our day, and
to end it well ... to focus
and pray –
asking God to bless us
with fortune and friends
in whatever we do
as we try to "fit in."
BUT it might be BETTER to just be free
if belonging is NOT the BEST we can be.

Perfect Plan

Are we morally vacant?
Without common sense?
Too much soap ...
not enough rinse?
If we could only hear
all the judgements
racing through our minds,
would we seek to change our views
or persist to be unkind?
There is nothing we can do, I guess –
except wait it out and PRAY.
I wonder if our Maker
must have planned it all this way.
After all,
would we seek forgiveness
if everyone were kind?
One day I'll know the answers
to these questions in my mind.

Ol' Nicodemus Here

Nicodemus – a Pharisee,
tried to understand
the difference between
our "spirit birth" and
the "simple flesh of man."
Like a mother giving birth
from water into flesh,
Jesus opens eternal life
through love – holy and blessed.
If we're wise enough to open our eyes
and believe He was born again,
we'll realize God's Only Son
has removed our every sin.
We're all a bit like good Ol' Nic –
trying hard to comprehend
the infinite LOVE of God
and a GIFT that never ends.

Tangents

I've drifted ... like you
through tangents in my life,
from a disappointed youth –
placing Jesus on a shelf ...
oftentimes with spite,
to help avoid the truth ... if I might.
I've often opted for "other things"
to fill up my weary soul,
but God understands His garden
needing time to grow.
Through sacred patience and perfect love,
He journeys right beside us.
And, one day we WILL know
how to claim our stage
and open wide the curtains ...
so God's truth isn't shadowed,
and His power is for certain!
God's NOT just "some story" personified
or some skeptic's raw illusion.
He is our Maker, Father, Savior and Friend –
The Journey to Joy!
This is my conclusion.

Aging With Grace

Once I thought I'd not grow old.
Obeyed the rules! Did what I was told!
And then one day my hair grew thin.
No longer a beauty like I had been.

My face was slender. My bones were weak.
The mirror summoned me to peek.
I covered my dread, so I could see
just what this world had done to me.

Wrinkles and lines grew everywhere ...
and around my mouth I even grew ... HAIR!
Spots of darkness dealt from the sun –
from years of laughter and having fun!

Life had aged me more than I knew.
My eyes were now gray instead of blue.
My smile – once lovely in my youth,
was emptied out ...
except for ONE TOOTH!

Faith Is My Choice

Faith is my choice ...
deliberately made.
It's a confidence shown –
unconditionally proving
God's presence has grown.
My vows are to Him,
to myself and to others –
for all my friends, sisters, brothers ...
where there is no retreat and
where hearts beat with assurance of an
ALWAYS OPEN DOOR!
Where encores never cease, and
LOVE is FOREVERMORE!

Have No Fear

Have no fear,
your God is here –
that faithful, devoted, Forever Friend,
OMNIPRESENT –
without end!
Let your every request reach His ear.
Listen closely, and you will hear.
His answers of love are right in view
with all the gifts He's given you!
Let Him be Master of all your dreams –
interests, passions ... everything!
He listens closely for your call –
when your dreams seem distant
or your needs seem small.
Please listen to His calming voice.
Let Him help you make each choice!

Listen

A legacy is what we leave
for others to esteem.
"Listen to your heart" –
not to things that "might have been."
Our lives are filled with such fantasies –
never delivering peace,
and often we're unaware
until it's time for us to leave.
Stop and listen now ...
for all those yearnings in your heart.
Leave a legacy worth the viewing –
like a "Priceless Piece of ART."

Satisfaction

When all big dreams have ended ...
when the edge of life has come,
when pain and joys have blended ...
and all your battles are won,
REST in your own imperfections.
Breathe slowly and try to stand tall!
Be proud to be God's creation, and
be grateful HE answered your calls!

Patriot's Prayer

God, be with us in times of need –
when we cry ... if we must bleed.
We believe in Your promises
and Your attending hands.
Restore our faith!
Reveal Your command!
We feel Your hope for humanity –
courageous, grateful and forever free!
Direct our steps with flags unfurled, and
lead us to PEACE throughout the world.

The Best of Me

God should have the best of me.
He deserves no less, indeed!
He only fashions with purpose –
and only for the good,
so would He want me to whine ...
give up on His Will,
or accomplish all I could?
Though I don't always know
the right way to go or
what He's expecting to see,
I'll continue to do the best I can.
He deserves the BEST of me!

Shekhinah

I will rest in knowing
that one day I'll reside
in that peaceful place
where Jesus pulls up His chair ...
RIGHT NEXT TO MINE!
I'll ask a thousand questions of Him,
and to each He will respond.
He'll speak to me so gently, and
I'll know I belong!
I will surely sing HIS PRAISES ...
grateful, loud and strong
as HE shares HIS INFINITE LOVE
every hour – all day long!

River

He is FOREVER ...
my fresh-flowing River!
Every morning and
when the sun goes down –
my source of holy warmth
where cleansing can be found.
A place for me to discover
what HIS LOVE truly means.
So, I listen to every sound
rippling from my River ...
saving each new mountain scene.
Even between the edges –
sometimes rough and wild,
He corrects my direction –
something you'd do for a child.
Though He lends me all essentials
to protect my soul's potential,
I often wonder ... WHY?
But then and again ... I am reconciled.
He is FOREVER my River!
I am the River's child.

Home

We could never, ever ask for more ...
God the Father opening His door,
folding our hands into His.
There is warmth all around!
NO CLOCKS in the room!
His Porchlight is ON
as He summons His moon!
He listens to His children
loving each new and perfect day!
I always imagined **Home** this way.

ABOUT ATMOSPHERE PRESS

Founded in 2015, Atmosphere Press was built on the principles of Honesty, Transparency, Professionalism, Kindness, and Making Your Book Awesome. As an ethical and author-friendly hybrid press, we stay true to that founding mission today.

If you're a reader, enter our giveaway for a free book here:

SCAN TO ENTER
BOOK GIVEAWAY

If you're a writer, submit your manuscript for consideration here:

SCAN TO SUBMIT
MANUSCRIPT

And always feel free to visit Atmosphere Press and our authors online at atmospherepress.com. See you there soon!

ABOUT THE AUTHOR

After years as a successful development professional for two outstanding nonprofits, **P.S. Glyckherr** is now retired and able to spend more time writing poetry and books for children.

She loves crafting ekphrastic lines for pieces of art and collaborating with other authors. Sharing life with her grandchildren has become one of her most favorite and rewarding experiences, and readers will find special references to her faith, family and friends in much of her writing.

www.ingramcontent.com/pod-product-compliance
Lightning Source LLC
LaVergne TN
LVHW041633070526
838199LV00052B/3329